PREHISTORIC HILLFORTS
in
DEVON

AILEEN FOX

DEVON BOOKS

First published in Great Britain in 1996 by Devon Books

British Library Cataloguing in Publication Data
CIP Catalogue Record for this book is available from the British Library

ISBN 0 86114 902 5

DEVON BOOKS
Official Publisher to Devon County Council

Halsgrove House
Lower Moor Way
Tiverton
Devon EX16 6SS
Tel: 01884 243242
Fax: 01884 243325

Cover photo: Aerial view of Clovelly Dykes (Site No.10)
(W. Horner, Devon County Council)
Back cover: Milber Down Camp, Newton Abbot by Peter Orlando Hutchinson
(Devon Record Office).

Printed and bound in Great Britain by Deltor Communications Ltd, Torpoint.

Contents

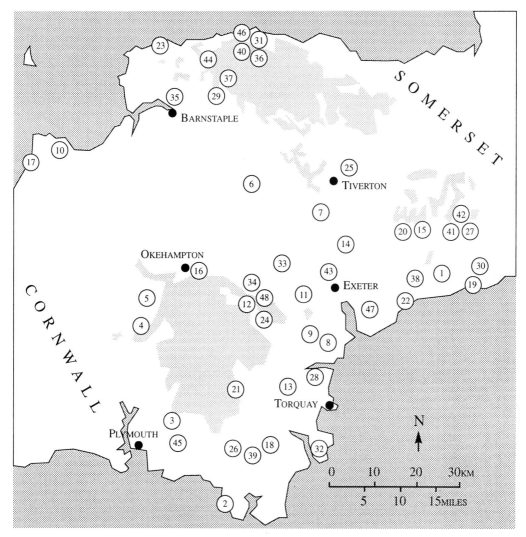

Fig. 1: *Hillforts in Devon: The circled numbers show the location of sites described in the Gazetteer. Land above 240m (800ft) is shaded.*

General Background Reading

References to reports and other studies relating to individual Devon hillforts can be found under the Gazetteer entries starting on page 20. The following titles are suggested for general background reading:

Barry Cunliffe. *Iron Age Britain*, Batsford Books/English Heritage, 1995
James Dyer. *Hillforts of England and Wales*, Shire Books, 1981
Aileen Fox. *South West England*, Thames and Hudson, 1964 (revised 1973)
Frances Griffith. *Devon's Past – An Aerial View*, Devon Books, 1988
Malcolm Todd. *The South West to AD1000*, Longmans, 1987

Preface

This booklet has been written in response to increased interest by the public in Devon's prehistoric past. It offers guidance to some of its most attractive visible remains, the fortified settlements of Celtic people known as hillforts, characteristic of the middle and late Iron Age (500 BC – AD50). It will try to explain their construction and their function and emphasizes their human interest. Above all the writer hopes it will tempt people to go and see some of the hillforts for themselves; they are listed and described in the Gazetteer.

The best time for visiting is when the bracken and undergrowth is minimal, in winter and spring, from January to June. Many of the sites are in public ownership or accessible by public footpaths and these are shown in the Gazetteer. For those hillforts in private ownership, permission should be asked whenever possible, though absentee landowners may be difficult to contact. Visitors should be careful to close gates, and avoid growing crops: dogs, even on a lead, are better left behind, particularly if there are sheep around.

The Gazetteer does not pretend to be a comprehensive list of hillforts in Devon; those omitted are either fragmentary, or difficult of access and some are simple ringworks similar to others included in the list.

Acknowledgements

The fieldwork on which the booklet is based was undertaken with Cyril, my late husband, from 1949 to 1963 and recorded in our field notebooks. I have recently revisited many sites assisted by Tony and Rosalind Payton or by my son George, to whom I am grateful for their help. Norman Quinnell kindly lent me several plans and also surveyed the fort entrance at Sidbury. I am also indebted to Martin Fletcher for plans made by the Royal Commission on the Historical Monuments of England at Exeter. Sue Rouillard has patiently redrawn all the hillfort site plans [Figs 12–37] whilst permission to reproduce reconstruction drawings and other figures has been kindly granted by a number of people who are acknowledged in the captions. Frances Griffith of Devon County Council and the Cambridge University Collection of Aerial Photographs have kindly provided the air photographs.

Finally, I owe a debt of gratitude to Simon Timms for readily accepting my offer to write about hillforts in the series to be published by Devon Books and for his constant interest and kind encouragement in its production.

Aileen Fox
August 1996

What is a Hillfort?

A hillfort is a defended settlement, enclosed by one or more ramparts built of earth dug from ditches, or built of stones; often the fortifications are conspicuous in profile in the landscape surrounding a hill-top, hence the name 'hillfort'. Excavation has shown that they were inhabited by peoples living in the 1st millennium BC, known to the Romans in Europe as well as in Britain as the Celts.

The sites were chosen for their natural defence, such as the steep slopes at the end of a spur like Hembury in East Devon or a hill-top like Dumpdon or the cliff edges of a coastal promontory like Bolt Tail. These were completed by the man-made defences, which were increased in size or number where it was easy for attackers to approach. The builders also elaborated and strengthened the ramparts at the entrance. The situation on a high point gave the advantage of a distant view of any threatening enemy movements. Each site was related to the surrounding land, where normally cultivation and grazing were carried on by the inhabitants under their chief in peace, together with others living in open settlements.

Plate 1: *Hembury (Site No. 20): this historic aerial view taken by H. Wykes in the 1930s whilst Miss Liddell's excavations were in progress gives an impression of the spur location of this East Devon hillfort and its massive rampart defences. Today the hillfort is considerably more wooded and overgrown with vegetation* (Devon Archaeological Society)

In Devon there are some hillforts that seem to scorn natural defences, being built on hill slopes as at Milber or on a plateau of level ground as at Clovelly Dykes. Their ramparts are not close-set defensively but spaced far apart, so that the fort consists of several interlocking enclosures. The entrances are simple, sometimes approached by an embanked roadway from the lower side or from the direction of a spring. Their design implies that the inhabitants were primarily pastoralists concerned with the management of their flocks and herds.

There are also many small simple enclosures, which, though on high ground, are not necessarily defensively sited. Most are circular between 60–150m in diameter. The single rampart and ditch were needed to protect the inhabitants from wind and rain and to keep out wild animals, rather than to repel an attack. Most are of a size to contain four or five round huts, probably housing a kin group of some twenty adults.

How to Find a Hillfort

The best way to start is with an Ordnance Survey map in the popular Land Ranger series, at a scale of 1:50,000 (one and a quarter inches to one mile), on which antiquities are marked and named in Gothic script. England is fortunate in having had an Ordnance Survey which from its early 19th century beginnings was directed to record and map antiquities carrying on the tradition set by early topographers like William Camden in the 16th century, or the military map-maker, General Roy in the 18th century.

At present, large hillforts are described on OS maps as 'Fort', the smaller as 'Enclosure'. Each can be identified by reference to the National Grid of kilo-metre squares; directions for its use are given in the margin of the OS maps. Guidance on selected sites and a brief description are given in the Gazetteer in alphabetical order, starting on page 20.

Place–names also help to identify a hillfort. The term 'bury' is the equivalent of the Anglo-Saxon 'burh' meaning fortification: Hembury, Sidbury, Blackbury, Prestonbury and Woodbury are conspicuous examples. Some names were applied to later English villages in the valleys as well as to the hillforts up above.The customary addition of the term 'Castle' therefore is strictly not neces-sary and may be confused with the later castles of the Middle Ages in the region. Likewise the term 'Camp' which is occasionally found, is misleading since it implies a temporary occupation of the site.

Aerial photographs can also reveal the location of a hillfort, even one previously unknown to the map-makers as Frances Griffith's work in Devon has shown.

From the air, a comprehensive view of a site and its place in relation to the surrounding countryside is available which is not possible on the ground; only tree cover can conceal the ramparts and ditches from the camera. If a site has been levelled, the defences may show up from the air as soil marks in a newly ploughed field, whilst a fort ditch will be revealed by a dark green marking in a pasture field or by variations in colour and growth of the crop in due season as it ripens. A selection of aerial photographs can be inspected at Devon County Council by appointment with the staff in the Devon County Sites and Monuments Register. Their interpretation needs an experienced archaeologist, for there are many pitfalls.

Why Build a Hillfort?

A chief and his dependents would decide to build a hillfort for the protection of the people, their dwellings, personal possessions, food stores and domestic animals when there was a threat of aggression. It would be designed as a conspicuous centre of tribal territory and would add to the prestige of its chief. The need was not felt in South West England until the late Bronze Age (1000–900 BC); previously, middle Bronze Age settlements as seen on Dartmoor were undefended, with small groups of round huts scattered in stone-lined fields or enclosed by a low pound wall. As time went on, a demand for weapons developed and a prolific bronze industry produced first rapiers, then cut-and-thrust heavy swords, socketed spearheads and axes as well as a variety of tools and personal ornaments. It is now that the first hillforts appeared as at Norton Fitzwarren in Somerset, though not yet identified in Devon. Long iron swords replaced bronze during the first millennium BC as the prestige weapons, though bronze was retained for decorative shields, scabbards, mounts and helmets for the aristocratic leaders. Another development in warfare in the Iron Age was the use of horses or rather sturdy ponies, controlled by their riders by bronze snaffle bits, or yoked in pairs to pull the pole of a lightweight two-wheeled chariot. Attackers could gain surprise by sudden movements; probably their aim was to carry off cattle, food stores and captives for slaves and not to acquire territory or to occupy the fort.

The answer to attack was defence. It is evident as at Hembury in East Devon that ramparts were increased in size and number, providing defence in depth: there was now another obstacle to be crossed as well a wider, deeper ditch and a final longer scarp to be scaled. There was also a new weapon, the ribbon sling, with a range of about 100m. The many pebble sling-stones found in Devon hillforts show that it was used by the defenders; throwing down-hill from the top of the rampart, they could out-range the attackers, as Sir Mortimer Wheeler pointed out long ago at Maiden Castle in Dorset.

How some Devon Hillforts were Built

It is unfortunate that very few Devon hillforts have been excavated by modern methods or on an adequate scale; we have to rely on the evidence provided from excavations at Hembury in East Devon (1930–35), at Stoke Hill Camp (1935), at Milber Down Camp (1937–38), at East Hill hillfort (1938), at Blackbury Castle (1952–54), at Woodbury Castle (1971), at Embury Beacon (1972–73) and again at Hembury (1980–83). References to these excavations may be found under the individual entries in the Gazetteer.

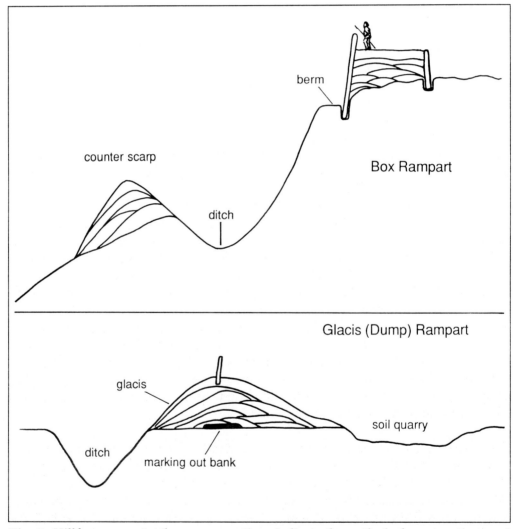

Fig. 2: *Hillfort ramparts: these cross sections indicate the method of construction used for a* box *rampart (above) and for a* glacis *rampart (below). In each case the hillfort interior is to the right. (Sue Rouillard)*

It was a considerable undertaking to start building a hillfort, committing the community's manpower for many months or even years ahead. Once a site with its natural advantages had been selected, the perimeter of the defences was marked out. This can sometimes be seen as a low bank, recorded in section beneath the main earth rampart at Blackbury and also surviving in the open in the unfinished portion of Cranbrook Castle.

The material for the rampart dug from the ditch varied according to the geology of the district, clay and sandstone from the Culm formations and yellow 'Fox mould', with broken chert from the Upper Greensand in East Devon for example. Turf and topsoil would be first stripped off and reserved for facing the rampart as at Embury Beacon or Stoke Hill. Flint nodules were similarly built into a kerb or low retaining wall beside the entrance to Blackbury. The problem was to prevent the rampart sliding into the ditch; this was solved by the use of timber uprights, both front and rear, forming a frame and linked horizontally on either side of the earth core creating a *box rampart* [Fig. 2] now known from Malcolm Todd's work at Hembury. A space, known as a *berm*, could also be left between the face of the rampart and the edge of the ditch; it is very evident at Cranbrook where it is one metre wide in front of the stone-faced rampart [Fig. 18].

The attempt to create a vertical rampart was soon abandoned in favour of a prolonged steep slope or *glacis*; successive loads of soil were tipped upwards to continue the incline of the ditch, forming a *dump rampart* [Fig. 2], a less laborious construction and easy to heighten if required. At its crest there might be a timber breast-work, discovered in section at Woodbury [Fig. 3], or some stonework, evident at Denbury. At Hembury in East Devon dump ramparts succeeded the original box rampart, no less than three of them on a major scale to block the easy northern approach, the outermost being unfinished.

In some hillforts soil for the ramparts was dug from an internal quarry, visible now as an extensive wide depression as at Membury, where there is no external ditch. At Sidbury where there are both an internal quarry and an external ditch, soil from the ditch was thrown down-hill to build a counter-scarp bank, in effect a second rampart.

Hillfort Entrances

The completed circuit of the rampart was designed as a deterrent to raiders. The main weakness was the gaps left for entrance gates and the associated causeways across the ditch, and consequently here extra effort and ingenuity were required. The ends of the ramparts were usually thickened on either side of a timber-framed wooden gate, closed by a horizontal bar internally. In some

Fig. 3: *A view of how the entrance gateway at Woodbury Castle (Site 47) might have looked when the hillfort was occupied.* (Mike Rouillard for the Devon Archaeological Society)

cases, extra deep post-holes suggest that the gate was bridged over enabling defenders to move along the top of the rampart unimpeded, as is evident at Hembury in East Devon and shown in the reconstruction drawings of Woodbury Castle [Fig. 3] and Loddiswell Rings [Fig. 4]. Another device was to build the rampart ends askew or slightly overlapping so that attackers had to turn and expose their sword arm as at Cadbury (outer gate) or at Dumpdon.

A widespread form was the inturned entrance [Fig. 5]. The objective here was by turning both rampart ends inward to create a bottle-neck in front of the gate, thereby penning the leading attackers within easy range of missiles and preventing the deployment of the main force from the causeway and beyond. Good examples of some 20m length can be seen at Cotley, Prestonbury and Dumpdon. Without excavation it is difficult to know the position of the gate; was it at the end of the inturn or at the first point where the rampart end could be bridged?

The only fully excavated entrances are at Hembury in East Devon, where Dorothy Liddell exposed the very large post-holes for massive timbers at both the west and east entrances. The gates were complicated by features relating to the early Neolithic occupation and also by the early Roman conversion of the

Fig. 4: *A reconstruction drawing of the entrance gateway at Loddiswell Rings.* (Piran Bishop for the Devon Archaeological Society)

fort gates for their own use, when a military detachment was garrisoned here AD 50–60 in the northern part of the fort.

The west entrance at Hembury [Fig. 6] was approached steeply up the 270m high hill, passing diagonally through the outer ramparts as a slightly sunk track, with a low bank on either side shutting off the ditch ends and supplemented by a palisade. The inner rampart then curved in behind the revetment of large posts below and in front of the gate, enclosing a 20m x 10m space, a target area for missiles. The entry, 2.5m wide, had a roughly metalled surface, in which wheel tracks 1.5m apart were detected. Groups of posts in four large post pits indicate that the rampart ends were bridged in front of the gate, whilst the ends of the inturn inside the gate were also revetted, probably for quick access to the bridge and to positions on the top of the rampart for the defenders. Similar designs for a target area in front of the gate are likely at Membury and Dumpdon, the latter being controlled from a fighting platform on the expanded end of the rampart.

Another device was to screen the gate by a defensible forecourt, known as a barbican, as seen at Blackbury [Fig. 5]. Here hornworks were added on either side of the entrance, converging at an outer gate, with an embanked passage-way leading towards the fort. Boringdon Camp near Plympton incorporates a similar design.

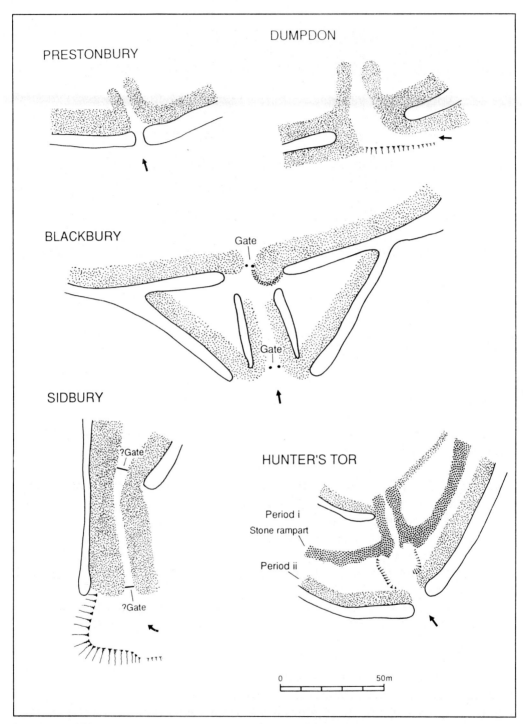

Fig. 5: *Hillfort entrances: five examples showing different arrangements for strengthening entrances which were the most vulnerable part of hillfort defences. Ramparts are shown by stippling and ditches in outline. (Sue Rouillard)*

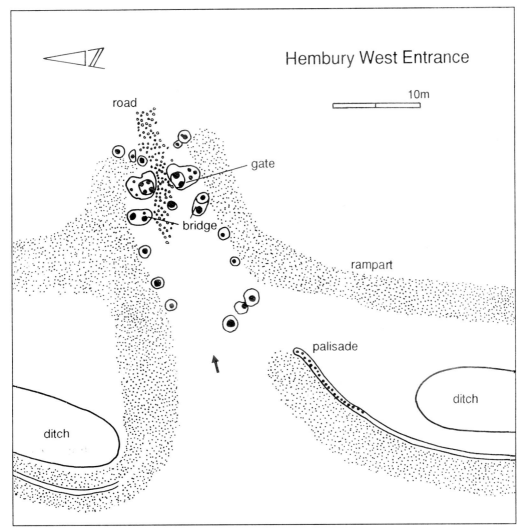

Fig. 6: *Excavation at Hembury has revealed detailed evidence of the layout of the hill-fort's west entrance. The solid circles indicate the location of post-holes to take upright timbers and the ramparts are stippled.* (Sue Rouillard)

At Sidbury [Fig. 5], the fort interior is entered from a steep embanked passage-way some 50m long, starting from a scarped platform and perhaps with an outer gate. It ends on level ground presumably at the main gate since the fort ditch on the south side terminates here. A hoard of sling-stones was found here-abouts in 1864 showing the entry was well defended.

Elaborate entrances are not found in the multiple-enclosure forts where a simple setting for the gate in a gap in the rampart is usual; sometimes this is coupled with an embanked droveway through the outworks as at Milber [Fig. 25], or by stone-faced embankments between two enclosures as at Hunter's Tor [Fig. 5], or

11

the deep winding holloway at Wooston Castle in the Teign valley [Fig. 37]. These would enable stock to be driven through cultivated ground without damaging the crops, or conversely to exclude them from the way into the fort interior. At Clovelly Dykes [Fig. 17] two primary central enclosures were entered from the ridgeway inland, the three additional enclosures from the opposite direction of the coast and of the springs where stock could be watered. These were screened by a substantial detached earthwork.

Hillfort Interiors

Even less is known about fort interiors than about their defences; such excavation as has taken place on Devon hillforts in the past sixty years has been very small-scale, consisting of test holes and narrow trenches, when only a bold area clearance was likely to yield results. At Danebury, a 5 hectacre hillfort on the chalk in Hampshire, Barry Cunliffe cleared a quarter of the interior before there was sufficient evidence for meaningful generalisation. He found a densely packed but well organised settlement with roadways kept clear, areas zoned for houses, storage pits and raised granaries, though with changes in layout during 600 years of occupation.

In the South West, the traditional house was circular, conspicuous as the stone-built hut circles on Dartmoor dating from the middle-late Bronze Age. Built in timber, with wattle and daub infilling, it persisted during the Iron Age as seen in the small enclosed settlement that preceded the Roman villa at Holcombe in East Devon. Nevertheless at the excavated site of Blackbury Castle the only domestic structure with a hearth and clay oven was found to be rectilinear; likewise at Woodbury and Embury Beacon post-holes recorded through excavation

Fig. 7: *Structures built inside hillforts included circular houses and raised rectangular granaries or stores. In this artist's impression of a hillfort interior, the rampart topped by a palisade can be seen in the background. (Redrawn from Elin M Jones' The Celts in the Iron Age)*

indicate rectilinear structures. No storage pits have been found, nor the groups of four or five post-holes characteristic of raised granaries, suggesting that corn-growing was less important than stock-raising in this area. It also seems likely that the fort interiors were not closely built up but much more excavation is needed to test this conclusion [Fig. 7].

Finds of iron slag at Blackbury and Hembury in East Devon testify to smithing, and possibly smelting from the iron ores obtainable on the Blackdown Hills. Repair of iron implements and weapons must have been frequently needed and a skilled blacksmith would have been a valuable and essential member of the community.

Life in a Hillfort

Although there is so little archaeological material as yet recovered from Devon hillforts, it is possible by using comparative finds from elsewhere and by using a disciplined imagination to attempt a sketch of life in an Iron Age hillfort. For most of the time it was far from glamorous, just plain hard work. Many of the humdrum tasks leave no archaeological trace, like the frequent chore of collecting firewood, increasingly from woods far away from the fort, or fetching water from the nearest stream in a skin bag or wooden pail. Actually very little water would be needed; cattle and ponies would be taken to the stream to drink and the inhabitants could satisfy their thirst or wash themselves at the same time.

It is unfortunate that acid soils from Devon have destroyed all remains of animal and human bone, so there are no details of the stock kept. From other places we know that the Iron Age people kept small, long-horned cattle similar to the present-day Dexter breed, sheep like the wild Soay sheep, the size and shape of a roe deer, as well as goats and lean pigs like the wild boar that is figured on Celtic metalwork. The stock would need constant minding and managing by herdsmen, probably with the help of dogs and boys. The elaborate earthworks at Clovelly Dykes [Fig. 17] suggest that at times a greater number of cattle were rounded up, sorted and segregated into separate enclosures, and singled out through a narrow embanked passage, probably at the time of the autumn slaughter. Some of the meat would be dried and salted to preserve it for the winter, and the hides stripped off for tanning as leather in a solution of oak bark. Hides as well as cattle are listed among the exports from Britain in the 1st century AD by the Greek author Strabo, so some may have been shipped from ports in the South West. Cattle normally would be penned or hobbled and milked in the outer enclosures which are a feature of South-Western hillforts like Milber or Burley Wood.

Corn growing was a necessity, the amount depending on the soil and the area cleared. Most days there would be an exodus from the fort to work in the fields:

according to the season, ploughing with a wooden ard with its iron tipped share, drawn by two yoked oxen, sowing spelt, barley and emmer varieties of wheat; beans were also cultivated. At harvest the ears of corn were cut with sickles, thrashed with flails and the grain stored. Then there would be the toil of grinding it, using a saddle quern and stone rubber to produce a coarse flour, which could be brushed and collected into a cloth. This would be used to make unleavened bread or porridge or a gruel: mixed with honey, it made the sweet bun found carbonised at the Glastonbury lake village in Somerset. Meat would be roasted on an open fire using spits or often heated stones and there might be an occasional feast, presided over by the chief and his warriors, sometimes after an animal's sacrifice dedicated to a god. In the season there were berries and herbs to be gathered, and hunting deer and wild boar for meat and skins, as well as fishing with nets in the rivers for trout, salmon and eels.

Fig. 8: *The elaborately decorated back of the bronze mirror excavated at Holcombe. A replica of this mirror, which is about 35cm in length (including handle), is on display in Exeter Museum.* (Philip Crompton, reproduced from *Proceedings of the Devon Archaeological Society*)

An expedition to the coast could collect shell-fish as well as a supply of sling-stones. From time to time, traders might visit the fort, bringing decorated pottery or metal objects to be exchanged for hides or grain.

For the women, spinning sheep's wool into thread would be a constant occupation; their stone or baked clay decorated spindle whorls were often lost, to be recovered by archaeologists. Woollen cloth, like a thick tweed, was woven on an upright loom, the warp held taut by clay or stone loom-weights. Vegetable dyes were used to produce the colourful clothing worn by the Celts described by the classical writers, and the blue from the woad plants was used for make-up. A noble woman might view the result in a polished bronze mirror hanging in her hut, like the decorated one from Holcombe in East Devon [Fig. 8]. Specialist craftsmen living within the fort would include the smith who would sharpen, repair and manufacture iron tools and implements. At the hillfort at St Mawgan in Pyder (Cornwall), a skilled bronze worker had his workshop with two stone-lined hearths and a furnace pit. Tin ore, a bronze ingot and crucibles were found

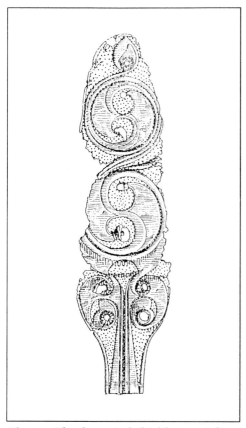

Fig. 9: *The decorated shield mount from Caerloggas hillfort at St Mawgan in Pyder is about 30cm long.* (from Aileen Fox's *South West England*)

on the floor as well as a decorated shield mount, showing what fine work could be produced locally at the end of the 1st century BC [Fig. 9]. This reminds us that though life in a hillfort was arduous and mainly concerned with food production and stock keeping, it was still an heroic society, dominated by the needs of the chief, his warriors and their women. They required swords in fine scabbards, shields, helmets and harness ornaments for display, *torcs* (neck rings), brooches and mirrors, decorated in the elaborated curvilinear style of Celtic art, characteristic of southern Britain in the middle and late Iron Age.

Hillfort Chronology

When did the phase of Iron Age civilisation in which hillforts were dominant begin in Devon and how long did it last? It is difficult to say due to the lack of datable material. Radio-carbon analysis of charcoals (C14 dating) from excavations has been little used in Devon and lacks the precision necessary for this period. The local tribes, known to the Romans as the *Dumnonii*, did not issue coins, though iron bars of regular weight and sizes were used for exchange in the 1st Century BC. A bundle of twelve such currency bars was found near a small hillfort overlooking the River Dart in Holne Chase in 1870 and another find of some seventy discovered recently in the vicinity of Milber Down hillfort.

Archaeologists have to rely on potsherds from the few hillfort excavations, principally of the attractive decorated type known as 'Glastonbury ware' (because it was first excavated at the Glastonbury lake village), with incised curvilinear and geometric patterns [Fig. 10]. Analysis of the clays has shown that such pots were made at various centres in Devon and Cornwall as well as in Somerset, and therefore were traded over a wide area from 300 BC onwards. In Devon, pieces have been found at Blackbury Castle, Cranbrook Castle, Embury Beacon, Hembury in East Devon and Milber hillforts, whilst at Blackbury Castle and

Fig. 10: *Pottery similar to these reconstructed examples of Glastonbury ware have been excavated on a number of Devon hillforts.* (Sue Rouillard; reproduced from John and Bryony Coles's *The Sweet Track to Glastonbury*)

Woodbury Castle plain wares of earlier middle Iron Age character indicate that some forts originated in the 4th century BC as did Hembury with its characteristic box rampart.

When did the Iron Age occupation come to an end? At Milber, the multiple enclosure fort had been abandoned well before the mid-1st century AD when three miniature animal bronzes were buried in the ditch filling [Fig. 11]. Other forts were probably abandoned before the Roman conquest but these must await identification through further investigation.

After the early Roman conquest of the West Country [c. AD 50–55], most Devon hillforts will have been given up. It was followed by 25 years of Roman military rule, based on the fortress of the Second Augustan legion at Exeter and with roads and small forts covering the hinterland. A detachment of troops was even

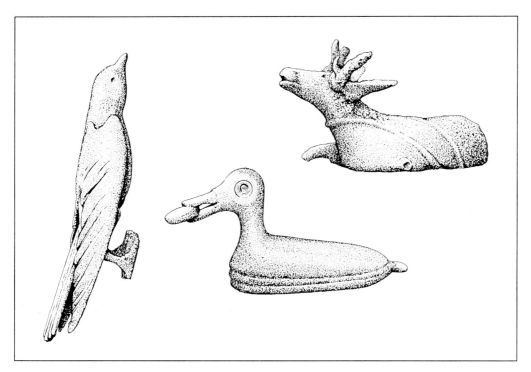

Fig. 11: *These bronze miniatures of a bird, stag and duck from Milber Down Camp are fine examples of prehistoric craftsmanship. They are on display in Torquay Museum. Drawn at actual size.* (Mike Rouillard for the Devon Archaeological Society)

stationed at Hembury hillfort in East Devon, probably to supervise iron-mining in the Blackdown Hills nearby.

After AD 75 the legion moved to Caerleon in South Wales, and a civil government was set up for the Dumnonii, in which Celtic chieftains from the hillforts could participate in the new administration. Some would have built small houses in the cantonal capital, Exeter (known as *Isca Dumnoniorum*), others modest dwellings in the country with rectangular timber houses replacing the former round huts as at Holcombe in East Devon, which later was to become a sophisticated Roman villa. It is not known whether some major hillforts were inhabited again during the 350 years of Roman rule, as they were in Somerset, (for example Brent Knoll), or whether like Cadbury and Congresbury they were re-fortified and occupied in the post-Roman era AD 400–700. Excavations have shown that people there obtained wine and oil imported from the Mediterranean in tall pottery vessels (*amphorae*) in the 5th and 6th centuries AD. These were traded widely in the South West. In Devon pieces have been found on the south coast at Bantham and Mothecombe, and also at High Peak, near Sidmouth, indicating that this much eroded fort was occupied and possibly built by a local ruler at this time before the Saxon intrusion in the 7th Century AD.

There was probably little change in the way of life in the smaller fortified settlements in mid and west Devon during the Roman administration or the succeeding centuries under native rulers in Dumnonia. Some will have survived as is known they did in Cornwall at Castle Gotha or Trethurgy, and some were newly built like Clannacombe, near Thurlestone, in South Devon.

A Future for Devon Hillforts ?

Ultimately all hillforts were abandoned but a proportion remain as features in the Devon landscape today. Their appearance has been altered by time. The profile of the defences has softened; the ramparts eroded by frost and rain, the ditches partly filled. They have become overgrown by scrub and trees, unless controlled by grazing. Some have been damaged by quarrying like Mockham Down, by stone robbing as at Hunters' Tor, others like Woodbury Castle cut

Plate 2: *Loddiswell Rings (Site No.26): this South Devon hillfort is owned by the Arundell Charity with the support of Devon County Council.* (F.M.Griffith, Devon County Council)

through by a highway. Others have been levelled and ploughed over by farmers and are now only visible on aerial photographs.

What can be done to protect the survivors? The State in the guise of English Heritage can take sites into guardianship as with Blackbury Castle in East Devon. Other hillforts are safe in the possession of the National Trust, as at Bolt Tail, Hembury (Buckfastleigh), Dolbury (Broadclyst) and Embury Beacon, or are owned by local authorities (for example Denbury and Boringdon Camp). English Heritage and local authorities can also enter into management agreements with landowners to preserve sites (as at Loddiswell Rings and East Hill).

Hillforts, like all ancient earthworks, can be protected by being scheduled as Ancient Monuments of National Importance. Their inclusion in the statutory Schedule means that the site may not be altered or damaged in any way without the prior consent of the Secretary of State, who is advised on such matters by English Heritage (23 Savile Row, London W1X 1AB). Scheduling also prohibits the use of metal detectors.

Further information on Devon hillforts is held in the Devon Sites and Monuments Register which is maintained by Devon County Council at County Hall, Exeter. Data recorded on the SMR is used to monitor planning applications so that the archaeological impact of any proposed development affecting prehistoric hillforts (and other archaeological sites) can be taken into consideration by local authorities. Planning policy is very much focused upon preserving important archaeological sites such as hillforts, but in instances where preservation is not possible, planning permission for new development would only be given on condition that any features or buried deposits which have to be destroyed are fully recorded by archaeological investigation.

The Devon Archaeological Society is also concerned with the preservation and maintenance of hillforts, having sponsored the major excavations at Hembury in East Devon and at Blackbury Castle in the past. It now produces a popular and inexpensive series of Field Guides for several hillforts and with the financial assistance of Devon County Council has set up Interpretation Panels at Woodbury Castle, Denbury and Loddiswell Rings. Members of the Society also offer practical help in clearing vegetation that threatens to obscure some hillforts and would welcome other volunteers to join them. The Devon Archaeological Society may be contacted c/o Royal Albert Memorial Museum, Queen Street, Exeter, EX4 3RX.

In these and other ways – such as by the publication of this booklet – it is hoped that the interest and understanding of owners and the general public will be aroused and sustained, for this can best ensure a future for the remarkable variety of Devon hillforts.

Gazetteer of Devon hillforts

This Gazetteer contains concise descriptions of forty-eight Devon hillforts listed in alphabetical order. Entries have been selected to cover the broad range of hillfort types, and simplified site plans for many hillforts have been included to give the reader an indication of their design and location. A general location map [Fig. 1] may be found on page 1. Each hillfort is identified by name, parish and location with National Grid Reference. The concise hillfort description is followed by a general note on access arrangements (marked by the symbol ⚑) and then, where appropriate, reference to further reading (marked by the symbol ✑). In these references, the abbreviation *PDAS* stands for *Proceedings of the Devon Archaeological Society*.

The site plans are diagrammatic. On the site plans, hillfort ramparts are indicated by solid black lines, whilst the former course of ramparts which have been levelled is shown by a thick dotted line. Narrow lines outline the course of hillfort ditches. Prehistoric entrances are shown by solid black arrows and probable entrances by unshaded open arrows. Site plans have North at the top of the page and contour heights are shown in metres as dash-dot lines.

In using the Gazetteer, the reader is asked to bear in mind the following points:

Hillfort conservation – Please help conserve Devon's hillforts for future generations to enjoy. Hillforts contained in this Gazetteer are scheduled as Ancient Monuments of National Importance under the *Ancient Monuments and Archaeological Areas Act 1979*. It is an offence to cause any deliberate damage to these scheduled monuments and no activities involving ground disturbance (eg excavation) or the use of metal detectors can be carried out without the express written consent of the Department of National Heritage.

Site Access – The majority of hillforts described in this Gazetteer lie on private land. Some guidance about access arrangements as they were found to exist in 1995 is given under each Gazetteer entry. A good number of hillforts are freely accessible to the public at reasonable times, but for others access is only possible to part of the site (eg where a public footpath crosses it) or after permission has been obtained from the landowner, whilst on some sites no public access is allowed. Readers are requested always to seek the landowner's permission before visiting any hillfort when they are in any doubt about public access (eg sites on farmland or in private woodland), and to follow the Country Code on all visits. *On no account should the inclusion of a hillfort in this Gazetteer be taken to mean that there is a formal right of public access to it.*

1. Blackbury Castle, Southleigh parish (SY 187 924) – Fig. 12

Blackbury is an important hillfort with an unusual entrance, excavated in 1952–54 by the Devon Archaeological Society. The oval enclosure of about 2 hectares now in open woodland straddles a 180m steep-sided Greensand ridge capped with clay and flints. It was defended by a substantial rampart and ditch, with one entrance facing the southern slopes; other gaps are recent. A triangular earthwork was added screening the gate – the so-called barbican entrance; it contained a central embanked passageway with a compartment on either side, probably used as stock pens.

Excavation showed that the main gate had been an imposing structure [Fig. 5]. The rounded rampart ends projected forward and were built up with flint nodules, retained by a timber palisade. Deep post-holes indicated the gate, probably with a bridge to link the ramparts. There was a second timber gateway at the entrance to the barbican. In the interior, the post-holes of a rectilinear hut were uncovered with a cooking pit nearby. Iron slag from the local limonite ores, whetstones and spindle whorls were found along with more than 1,200 sling stones. The pottery included decorated Glastonbury ware and some earlier plain Iron Age wares indicating that the fort was in use from the early 3rd century BC onwards.

⚑ In care of English Heritage. Free public access with car park. Signposted from A3052 Sidford-Colyford road and from the B3174.

📖 Young, A. and Richardson, K. 'Report on Excavations at Blackbury Castle', *PDAES* 5(1953–58), 43–67

2. Bolt Tail Hillfort, Malborough parish (SX 669 396) – Plate 3.

A fine example of a promontory fort or 'cliff castle', built at the end of Bolt Tail. The headland is surrounded by steep cliffs (between 20–60m high) of hornblende schist which are subject to erosion and falls. A landing however is possible from Bigbury Bay at the small sandy beach at Hope Cove nearby.

The fort is defined by a single rampart up to 2–5m high across the narrowest part of the promontory, cutting off 5 hectares of undulating ground. It overlooks a dry valley to the east across which all-comers must approach uphill in full view of the defence.

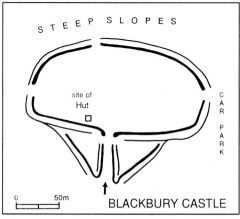

Fig. 12: *Blackbury Castle*

Plate 3: *Bolt Tail hillfort (Site No.2): a fine promontory fort on the South Devon coast* (F.M.Griffith, Devon County Council)

The entrance is inturned and the ramparts are heightened on either side where there are traces of an outer ditch from which the extra soil was dug. The stone wall along the base of the rampart is modern. The interior has been ploughed in the past and the sites of any prehistoric dwellings have been obliterated.

Ⱡ Owned by the National Trust. Accessible by the Coast Path from the east, or from Hope Cove where cars can be parked.

🖙 Devon Archaeological Society *Bolt Tail* Field Guide No. 8(1992)

3. Boringdon Camp, Sparkwell parish (SX 544 596) – Fig. 13

A medium sized hillfort on a rounded 140m high hilltop east of the lower Plym valley and close to the Plympton–Shaugh Prior road. The earthwork is circular, enclosing about 2 hectares, but the rampart and ditch

Fig. 13: *Boringdon Camp*

have been much reduced by ploughing; at best the bank is one metre high. The entrance facing south is screened by two projecting banks which converge to form a barbican-like forecourt and an outer entrance. Other gaps in the rampart are recent.

⚲ In a pasture field owned by South Hams District Council with public access by footpath and stile from adjoining Forestry Commission plantation.

🐚 Slater, W. and Pearson, T. 'A Survey of Boringdon Camp', *PDAS* 43 (1985), 112–15

4. Brent Tor hillfort, Brentor parish
(SX 471 804) – Plate 4

Brent Tor is an isolated hill of volcanic origin, 300m high and visible for many miles around; it is crowned by St. Michael's church founded in the twelfth century by Tavistock Abbey, restored in the late nineteenth century.

The Iron Age fortifications are visible on the slopes facing north-east and south, consisting of two close-set ramparts and ditches with an inturned entrance worn and spread. A third line with stone facing lower down the slope appears to be a later property boundary. Most of the site has been dug over for manganese.

⚲ Accessible by footpath from the Lydford–Lamerton and Tavistock roads with car park adjoining.

🐚 Silvester, R. 'The relationship of first millennium settlement to the upland areas of Dartmoor', *PDAS* 37(1979), 176–90

Plate 4: *Brent Tor (Site No.4): the remains of the hillfort ramparts are visible around this volcanic landmark on the west side of Dartmoor. The church on the summit was built in the Middle Ages* (Cambridge University Collection)

5. Burley Wood hillfort, Bridestowe parish (SX 495 875) – Fig. 14.

An interesting complex fort of multiple enclosures of two or three periods, and a south-western type. It is situated on a steep-sided knoll 220m high at the end of a spur three kilometres south-west of Bridestowe.

The main enclosure with an inturned entrance occupies the crest, now covered with a plantation. It was probably supplemented, or perhaps preceded, by two small cross-banks 30m apart across the saddle to the south, now much ploughed down in a pasture field.

The hillfort was extended southwards by an annexe containing a small secondary enclosure; it was entered from the west and the direction of a spring, so may have been designed for livestock. Finally the whole complex was re-fortified by a massive rampart and ditch further south across the spur and up the slope, with its ends secured on the steep slopes to Foxcombe and a tributary stream. The entrance at the east end is probably original, the central gap more recent. There is also a Norman motte and bailey castle in the dense woodland, east of the main hillfort.

🚶 Privately owned. Parking is possible at Combebow off the old A30 to the north, from where a walk of 25 minutes up a public footpath leads to a field gate and the outworks.

📖 Fox, A. 'South-Western Hill-Forts' in Frere, S.S. (ed.) *Problems of the Iron Age* (1961), 47–49

6. Burridge Hillfort, Chawleigh parish (SS 742 125)

A circular enclosure 85m in internal diameter, situated on the edge of the 180m high upland three kilometres east of Chawleigh, above the steep wooded fall to the Little Dart river. It was defended by a single rampart 1.5m. high and a ditch with a counter-scarp bank on the west, all rather denuded. The entrance faces south-west. In grass but formerly ploughed. Such simple ringworks are not dateable and could have been made for livestock as well as for human habitation.

🚶 Privately owned. Public footpath from the Burridge-Cheldon road skirts the north side of the ramparts.

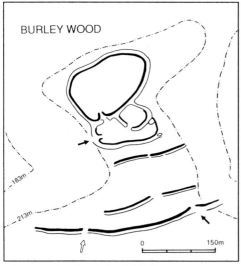

Fig. 14: *Burley Wood hillfort*

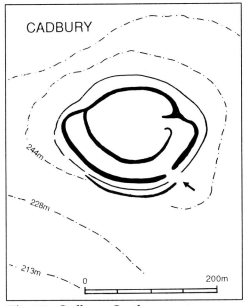

Fig. 15: *Cadbury Castle*

7. Cadbury Castle, Cadbury parish
(SS 913 053) – Fig. 15.

A medium-sized hillfort situated on a steep-sided rounded hilltop 253m high, west of the Exe valley, and about quarter of a mile from Cadbury church; there are fine views in all directions.

Cadbury hillfort appears to be a work of two periods; the first, a circular construction of about one hectare enclosed by a single rampart and ditch, which have been partly levelled and ploughed down on the south side. It has an inturned entrance facing east, also lowered by ploughing. The hillfort was enlarged to one and a half hectares by a bigger rampart and ditch with a counter-scarp bank built 10–12m away, forming a well-defended semi-circular outer enclosure. A new entrance was made facing south-east, the easiest approach; all-comers needed to turn right and pass along below the inner rampart to reach the old inturned entrance to the interior of the hillfort.

A remarkable well shaft was discovered in 1847 on the hilltop, 17m deep into the Permian sandstone; at 6–8m a collection of Roman jewelry was found, consisting of bronze bracelets, beads and rings of the 3rd and 4th centuries AD. It was probably a votive deposit to a local god and it is possible that a Romano-British timber temple stood nearby.

ᛉ Privately owned. Access by lane and public footpath from Cadbury–Thorverton road. The Roman objects from the well are displayed at Fursdon House, which is open to the public in the summer.

🖎 Fox, A. 'Roman objects from Cadbury Castle', *Transactions of the Devonshire Association* 84(1953), 105–14.

8. Castle Dyke, Ashcombe Parish
(SX 921 770)

A circular enclosure about 120m in diameter in woodland on Little Haldon Hill at an altitude of 220m. It is fortified by a single bank 1.5m high and a ditch with a causeway and entrance gap facing south-east. The level interior has been partly cleared but the perimeter is very overgrown.

ᛉ Privately owned. Located at the crossroads on the road from the B3192 to Luscombe Castle.

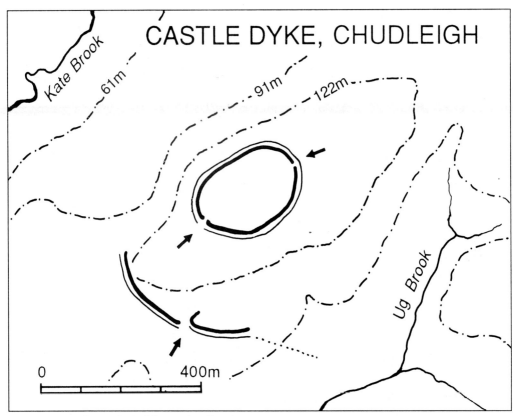

Fig. 16: *Castle Dyke hillfort, Chudleigh*

9. Castle Dyke hillfort, Chudleigh parish (SX 875 787) – Fig. 16.

A substantial hillfort with an external crossbank, situated on the summit of a 130m hill between the Kate Brook and the Ug Brook in the landscaped parkland of Ugbrooke House, a castellated mansion built for Lord Clifford in 1763–66 by Robert Adam.

The oval hillfort enclosure of 300x200m is defended by a substantial rampart and ditch; the interior has been regularly ploughed. There are two entrances, from the north-west where there is a causeway between the ditch ends and a slight inturn of the rampart, and from the south-east where the rampart ends are raised and thickened, though the ditch continues unbroken and may have been bridged.

The Castle Dyke, from which the hillfort takes its name, is an impressive cross-bank and ditch which starts on the north 40m from the edge of the steep fall to the Kate Brook and continues across the saddle and down the southern slope towards the Ug Brook, ending as a holloway. There is a central entrance with an inturn on the lower side, now spread by ploughing. The Dyke presumably defended a stock enclosure or an area of cultivation belonging to the hill-fort, fenced in by lateral palisades: it is similar to others at the multiple-enclosure hillforts at Burley Wood and Prestonbury [Figs 14 and 30].

𝑥 Privately owned. No public access.

10. Clovelly Dykes, Clovelly parish (SS 311 234) – Fig 17, Front cover and Plate 5.

Clovelly Dykes is the most impressive set of prehistoric earthworks in Devon: in its final form, it consists of over three kilometres of banks and ditches, defining and defending six enclosures covering eight hectares. It is situated three kilometres inland from the coast at Clovelly, adjoining the A39 and the B3237 main roads. Unlike most hillforts it has no natural defence, though sited at a high point (200m) on the coastal plateau. Some small streams rise nearby and there is access by ridgeway from several directions. The interior is now maintained as pasture by East Dyke Farm.

The hillfort plan

The primary enclosures: air photographs (Plate 5) indicate that the hillfort is not all of one period. The two concentric central enclosures appear to be the earliest and are likely to be where people lived. The entrances are on the east side, where the ends of the outer ditch are intact; other gaps in the defences are recent.

The secondary enclosures: the hillfort was greatly enlarged by the building of three strip-like enclosures on the west and north, most probably for stock, and another crescent-shaped on the east side. These now contain the modern buildings, East Dyke and

Plate 5: *Clovelly Dykes (Site No.10) has the most impressive hillfort earthworks in Devon* (F.M.Griffith, Devon County Council)

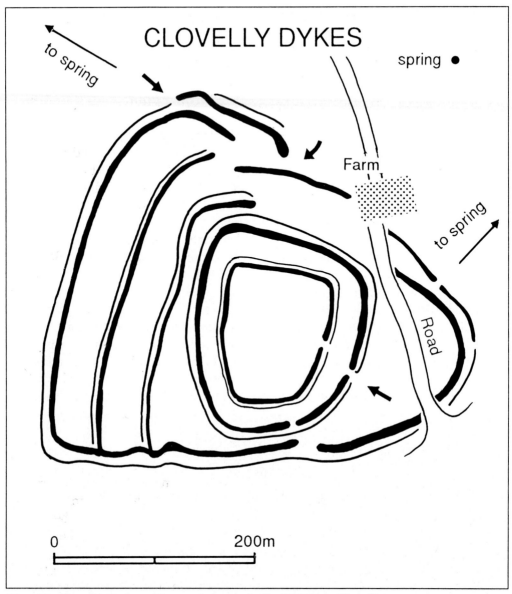

Fig. 17: *Clovelly Dykes. The road shown is the B3237 to Clovelly.*

Dyke Green farms, as well as some of the adjoining B3237 road. New extra entrances were provided from the north-west/north-east, in the direction of the springs, screened by a detached line of earthwork with a knobbed terminal. From here there was access to all the strip enclosures, including a narrow 2m wide passage-way between the edge of the ditch and the knobbed rampart end. This would provide a vantage place for oversight of the movement of stock, for singling and even for slaughter. No excavation has taken place at the Dykes; a blue glass bead of Iron Age type was found by a previous farm tenant.

Interpretation: The reason for multiple enclosures such as Clovelly Dykes can never be wholly known, but it seems likely they were made to contain and to manage large numbers of livestock, as well as to protect them from wild animals or cattle raiders. Groups of beasts could be separated for grazing, milking, mating or slaughter, whilst the narrow passageway suggests it was a place for a gate and single file control. Cattle need water and significantly the new entrances face towards the springs on the seaward side. Since there are no comparable hillforts on the coastal tract between Bideford and Hartland, Clovelly Dykes probably became a recognised tribal centre and a market place for the district. An export trade is also a possibility since Strabo, a Greek author writing in the 1st century BC, lists cattle and hides as well as corn, metals and hunting dogs among the goods exported from Britain (*Geographia* IV, 5.2).

🏛 Privately owned. Permission to visit may be requested from East Dyke Farm.

🖐 Fox, A. 'Hill-slope forts and related earthworks in South West England and South Wales' *Archaeological Journal* 109(1953), 10–14.

11. Cotley Castle, Dunsford parish (SX 860 896) – Plate 6.

A medium-sized hillfort on a 220m hilltop of the Haldon ridge above the south-facing slopes to a lateral valley, opening eastwards.

It is strongly defended by a single rampart and ditch, and has an impressive inturned entrance 19m, long, reached by a 7m wide causeway between the ditch ends on the south side. The interior is covered by a dense conifer plantation.

🏛 Privately owned. Located three kilometres south of Longdown; a track skirts the south side of the hillfort.

12. Cranbrook Castle, Moretonhampstead parish (SX 738 890) – Fig. 18.

Situated on the south side of the Teign gorge above Fingle Bridge at a height of 320m. Cranbrook is the best example of a stone-built hillfort in Devon, though apparently unfinished and damaged by stone robbing. The hill is part of the Culm formations.

The hillfort consists of a large circular enclosure of 2.8 hectares, defended by a substantial stone faced rampart 2m high, separated from a steep-sided ditch by a distinct berm 1m wide; on the south side there is an outer rampart and ditch, extending to screen the west entrance. On the north side the defences were not completed; a low bank and some stone heaps indicate the intended line and the nearby field walls show where other stones have gone.

There are two entrances, both simple gaps on west and east, much enlarged by stone robbing. A third entrance at the south-east end of the outer rampart is probably related to

Plate 6: *Cotley Castle (Site No.11): an aerial view of the hillfort after tree felling. The site has since been replanted* (Cambridge University Collection)

an earlier embanked enclosure which was put out of use when the main defences were built. Limited excavation in 1901 recovered some Iron Age pottery dating from after 200 BC, slingstones and a piece of a quern.

It can never be known why this well-built hillfort was not finished; perhaps the defences were started to meet a threatened attack which did not eventuate. The inhabitants then felt that the labour of ditch digging and stone collecting was excessive and a timber palisade was substituted to prevent domestic or wild animals from intruding.

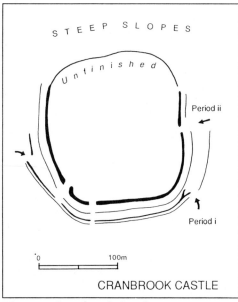

Fig. 18: *Cranbrook Castle*

ꙮ Privately owned. Access by car on narrow roads from Moretonhampstead or Easton. On foot, uphill by track three quarters of a mile from Fingle Bridge. Footpath to site is signposted.

🖙 Collis, J. 'Cranbrook Castle, Moretonhampstead. A New Survey', *PDAS* 30(1972), 216–221
  Collis, J. 'Cranbrook Castle Revisited', *PDAS* 37(1979), 191–94
  Silvester, R.J. and Quinnell, N.V. 'Unfinished hillforts on the Devon moors', *PDAS* 51(1993),25–27

13. Denbury hillfort, Torbryan parish (SX 816 685) – Fig. 19.

This wooded hillfort crowns the 150m high end of Denbury Down, a little ridge of Devonian limestone and of volcanic spilite to the west of Denbury village. It is conspicuous on the skyline from many directions in the surrounding undulating countryside.

The hillfort was strongly defended by two close-set ramparts and a deep ditch on the east and south sides. The lines of these diverge to form an outer enclosure on the west side, a later addition perhaps designed as a livestock enclosure. Its low bank is unconsolidated and probably was unfinished. On the north side the defences have been ploughed down leaving a single scarp, and are overlain in part by hedgebanks.

The outer enclosure was entered from the southern slopes through a 10m gap between the offset rampart ends, now complicated by a later drainage ditch. At the main hillfort, the western rampart ends were inturned to form a short defensive passage-way in front of the original wooden gate.

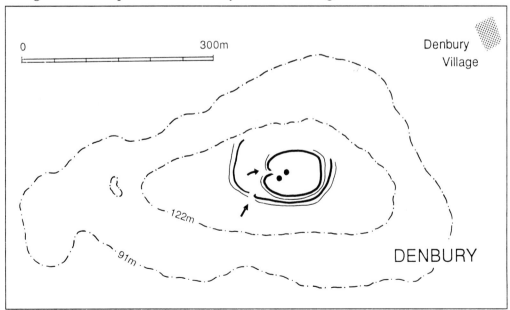

Fig. 19: *Denbury hillfort. The barrows in the interior are shown as black dots.*

The wooded interior is currently obscured by undergrowth which will be cleared eventually. In the centre are two large mounds, almost certainly Bronze Age barrows, and likely to cover cremation burials. Their irregular shape is due to ancient ploughing which has also destroyed the back slope of the rampart. No excavation has taken place but early forms of the place name *Defnasburh* and *Deveneberie* meaning 'fort of the Devon people' suggest it was an important place inhabited in post-Roman times as well as in the Iron Age.

✦ Owned by Devon County Council. Access by lane and footpath from the bye road leading west from the village. Interpretation panels on the site.

🔗 Probert, S.J. and Dunn, C.J. 'Denbury Camp, Torbryan parish: a new survey by the Royal Commission on the Historical Monuments of England', *PDAS* 50 (1992), 53–60

14. Dolbury hillfort, Broadclyst parish (SS 973 004)

In the grounds of Killerton House, formerly owned by the Acland family and now by the National Trust.

On the 120m high hilltop above the gardens there is part of the rampart and ditch of a small circular hillfort surrounding the recent beech clump. About two-thirds of the perimeter is visible, the remainder being destroyed when the trees were planted. The

entrance is on the north-west side facing the steep slopes to the river Culm. There is good visibility in all directions.

✦ Owned by the National Trust. Access on foot from Killerton House by gates at the top of the garden, or by footpath from the south-east through the park. NT car park at Killerton.

15. Dumpdon hillfort, Luppitt parish (ST 175 041) – Fig. 20.

This hillfort, crowned by a beech clump, is conspicuous in the landscape north and east of Honiton. It was built on the 260m high southern end of a steep-sided ridge of Upper Greensand between the river Otter and the Luppitt brook. The position is commanding with fine views in all directions.

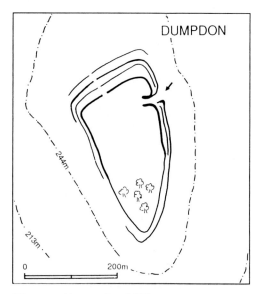

Fig. 20: *Dumpdon hillfort*

The triangular hillfort, 2.6 hectares in extent, was defended by two substantial ramparts and ditches 30m apart on the northern side, controlling the only easy line of approach, and by single ramparts on the east and west sides which diminish in size towards their southern meeting point beyond the beech clump.

The inturned entrance adjoins the north-east angle [Fig. 5]; the track from the north turns sharply on to a broad causeway between the ditch ends screened by low banks, which, like the west gate at Hembury, were probably revetted with timber. The thickened end of the southern rampart suggests it was a fighting platform covering the approach as well as the target area in front of the gate. The gate presumably was at the end of the 20m long inturn. Other gaps are recent.

Excavations in 1990 by Professor Malcolm Todd at the southern end of the hillfort showed that the defences here were unfinished and there were no traces of occupation in this part of the hillfort.

🏃 Owned by the National Trust. Access from the A30 via Langford Bridge and then by narrow lanes. Small parking area below hillfort. Best to visit in spring before the bracken has grown.

📖 Devon Archaeological Society *Dumpdon* Field Guide No.9 (1994)
  Todd, M. 'The hillfort of Dumpdon', *PDAS* 50 (1992), 47–52

16. East Hill hillfort, Okehampton Hamlets parish (SX 604 941)

A small promontory fort on the edge of Dartmoor, south of Okehampton. It was described by its excavator, John Brailsford in 1939 as 'near Okehampton station', which is now closed. The site is at the end of the East Hill ridge 300m high, and is naturally defended by the steep wooded slopes to the East Okement river and the Moor Brook.

The hillfort was defined by a single rampart, probably stone-faced and surviving 2-3m high, and a wide, flat bottomed ditch, which curve across the end of the ridge but stop short of the steep slopes; the northern segment has probably been ploughed out. The entrance faces west and is central. The small-scale 1939 excavation showed that the rampart end here was neatly faced with eleven courses of small slabs and that there was a (? previous) palisade trench in the passage to the gate. Nothing dateable was found. The site is now rough pasture and the entrance has been widened for farm vehicles.

🏃 Privately owned. Accessible on foot from the bye road to Lower Halstock Farm and ¹/₂ mile over East Hill.

📖 Brailsford, J.W. 'Excavations at the Promontory Fort near Okehampton Station', *PDAES* 3 (1937–47), 86–9

Plate 7: *Embury Beacon (Site No.17), showing the short lengths of rampart surviving on the cliff edge. Most of the hillfort has been lost to cliff erosion* (F.M.Griffith, Devon County Council)

17. Embury Beacon hillfort, Hartland parish (SS 216 196) – Plate 7.

Embury Beacon was a promontory hillfort on the 150m high cliffs on the west coast, nine kilometres south of Hartland Point. Erosion has destroyed all but a short length of its two ramparts 40–60m apart. A rescue excavation in 1972–3 recorded the structure of the dump ramparts and a gully, hearths and post-holes of a rectilinear building from which some decorated (Glastonbury style) pottery was recovered, as well as whetstones and shale spindle whorls. These are important as demonstrating this coastal promontory fort is contemporary with those inland.

𝄃 Owned by the National Trust. Accessible from the Coast Path. An exposed site.

𝇌 Jefferies, J.S. 'An Excavation at the Coastal Promontory Fort of Embury Beacon, Devon', *PDAS* 40(1979), 136–56

18. Halwell Camp, Halwell parish
(SX 784 532)

A circular enclosure about 80m in diameter, situated on 190m high ground east of Halwell village astride the B3207 Dartmouth road, which has cut through the southern segment of the hillfort. The remains consist of a substantial rampart 2m high with a ditch ploughed in but visible as a depression. Entrance uncertain: a gap facing north is probably recent.

The earthwork is very similar to Stanborough Camp, visible some two kilometres away to the south–west, and both are of Iron Age character.

It is possible that Halwell was reused as a Saxon fortification against the Danes in the late 9th or 10th century AD, as it is mentioned in an Anglo-Saxon document, the *Burghal Hidage*, as a burh together with Exeter, Pilton and Lydford.

𝔛 Privately owned. Visible where it is bisected by the B3207 Dartmouth road.

19. Hawkesdown Camp, Axmouth parish (SY 263 914)

A well-defended hillfort of medium size, situated on a steep-sided wooded hill 125m high overlooking the Axe estuary, north-east of Axmouth village. The soil is calcareous over the Upper Greensand.

The principal defence is a massive rampart 4m high and a ditch in places over 6m deep, facing the only level approach from the east. These continue westward along the northern side facing Stedcombe House, diminishing slightly. On the west and south sides the rampart survives as a substantial field bank, and the ditch has been partly filled in. On the south side there is a recent track along the ditch and through the rampart into the interior of the hillfort, now used for pheasant rearing. The main entrance was at the south-east angle, where the ditches terminate and the end of the eastern rampart is expanded; the passageway is now blocked by a hedge-bank. It is possible that there was a postern gate at the north-west angle, now obscured by hedgebanks, though the slopes from here towards the river are very steep.

100 metres east of the hillfort there is the remains of a substantial bank across the ridge, now a field boundary: it probably defended an outer enclosure. A recent find here of seven small lead sling bullets (*glandis*) of mid 1st century AD type is highly suggestive of an early Roman attack.

𝔛 Privately owned. No public access.

🕮 Holbrook, N. ' Roman lead shot from near Hawkesdown', *PDAS* 47(1989), 117–18

Hutchinson, P.O. 'Antiquities in south-eastern Devon', *Transactions of the Devonshire Association* 2 (1867–68), 378–79

20. Hembury hillfort, Payhembury parish (ST 113 030) – Fig. 21, Plate 1.

Hembury, the most impressive and important of the Devon hillforts, is situated at the southern end of a 240m high ridge protruding from the Blackdown Hills some five kilometres north-west of Honiton. The site commands extensive views over the Otter river valley and its tributaries, the Tale to the west, the Wolf to the east, with a glimpse of the sea on a clear day to the south. The underlying rock is the Upper Greensand capped with a calcareous yellow soil (Fox mould) and pockets of chert. Excavations by Dorothy Liddell for the Devon Archaeological Society took place in 1930–35 and by Professor Malcolm Todd in 1980–83.

The first defence of the three hectare enclosure on the level top of the ridge consisted of a timber-faced box rampart and ditch. This was subsequently heightened and converted into a glacis (dump) rampart and two others down-built from the ditches to provide defence in depth (Fig. 2). The defences follow the contour round the steep hillsides but across the spur, where there was an easy line of approach, the earthworks were greatly enlarged and became virtually unscaleable. The outermost rampart here was not completed.

There were two inturned entrances on the west and east sides approached by embanked causeways across the ditch ends which excavations show to have been revetted with large timbers to form a target area in front of the gate (Fig. 6). The ends of the inner rampart were connected by a bridge over the gate for the benefit of the defenders armed with pebble slingstones, many being found in the area.

Little is known about the living area inside the hillfort, now covered with bracken; finds of decorated (Glastonbury style) pottery, glass beads and stone spindle whorls are consistent with occupation from the 3rd century BC though the box rampart suggests an earlier origin in about 400 BC. The hillfort was probably abandoned

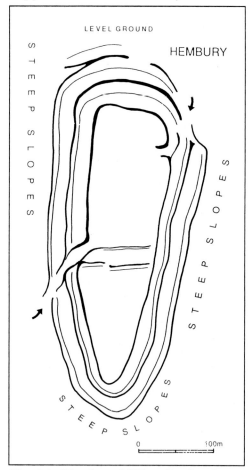

LEVEL GROUND

HEMBURY

STEEP SLOPES

STEEP SLOPES

STEEP SLOPES

0   100m

Fig. 21: *Hembury hillfort, Payhembury*

before a detachment of the conquering Roman army occupied the northern end, about AD 50. Two small cross-banks and ditches defend the southern side of their 2.5 hectare enclosure, entered through the Iron Age gates, where new timbers were inserted. Professor Todd's excavations revealed that the soldiers had erected rectangular timber buildings including a workshop (*fabrica*). The Roman occupation was brief, probably from AD 50–60, as shown by Claudian coins, Samian and other pottery, and so contemporary with the early legionary fortress at Exeter. The Roman garrison at Hembury may also have supervised iron-working in the Blackdown Hills nearby. The Roman name for the site was probably *Moridunum* though this is disputed.

Miss Liddell's excavation in 1930–35 disclosed that there had been an extensive earlier, Neolithic occupation of the hilltop, dated by radiocarbon analysis of charcoal fragments to 3330–3000 BC. This Neolithic site was defined by causewayed ditches at the southern end of the spur and around the area of the later, Iron Age east entrance but no Neolithic features are visible today.

🏃 Privately owned. Access by public footpath from A373 and from the bye road to Dunkeswell north of the hillfort where there is convenient parking and a level track to the east entrance. Best to make a visit in the spring before the bracken has grown. Excavation finds are in the Royal Albert Memorial Museum in Exeter.

📖 Devon Archaeological Society *Hembury* Field Guide No.5 (1989)

Todd, M. 'Excavations at Hembury, Devon: A Summary Report', *Antiquaries Journal* 64(1984), 251–68 (also contains references to Miss Liddell's excavations)

21. Hembury Castle, West Buckfastleigh parish (SX 726 684) – Fig. 22.

A large hillfort with a Norman motte and bailey castle later inserted at one side. It is situated at 170m on rising wooded ground between the River Dart and the Holy Brook about three kilometres north-west from Buckfast Abbey.

The enclosure of some three hectares is defended by a rampart and deep ditch with a substantial counter-scarp bank, best preserved along the northern side. The entrance is on the lower southern side approached by a 8m wide causeway across the ditch. The interior has recently been cleared of

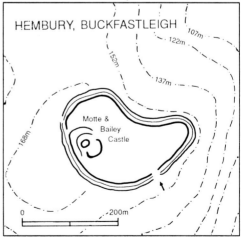

Fig. 22: *Hembury Castle, Buckfastleigh*

undergrowth by the owners, the National Trust.

The small motte and bailey castle was constructed in the 11th or 12th century AD on the west side of the prehistoric enclosure where the adjoining Iron Age defences were thickened and heightened. A timber tower was probably built in the central hollow of the motte, similar to that at Loddiswell Rings (page 40). Nothing is known of the Norman ownership of this castle.

⚔ Owned by the National Trust. Accessible from narrow bye road from Buckfast to Holne Chase. There is a small parking place nearby.

🐌 Griffith, F. *Devon's Past – An Aerial View* (1988), 9, Fig 3.

22. High Peak hillfort, Otterton parish (SY 103 859)

There is only a small fragment surviving of the hillfort on the crest of Peak Hill, two kilometres west of Sidmouth; the remainder has been destroyed by coastal erosion and falls from the unstable 150m high cliffs of Upper Greensand.

Excavations in 1961 by Mrs Pollard showed that the site was defended on the landward side by a rampart scarp and ditch with a small outer rampart facing east. No Iron Age finds were recovered from the occupation layers but radiocarbon dates of the late 5th century AD came from charcoal associated with sherds of imported Mediterranean amphorae (wine jars) which came from ditch filling and cooking holes. It appears that this hillfort was of post-Roman construction (see page 17), although some early Neolithic occupation of the site is also attested. Finds in the Royal Albert Memorial Museum in Exeter.

⚔ Privately owned. Accessible by a steep ascent from the Coast Path. An exposed site.

🐌 Griffith, F. *Devon's Past – An Aerial View* (1988), 64, Plate 50.
   Pollard, S. H. M. 'Neolithic and Dark Age Settlements on High Peak, Sidmouth, Devon', *PDAS* 23 (1966), 35–59
   Pollard, S. H. M. 'Radiocarbon dating. Neolithic and Dark Age Settlements on High Peak, Sidmouth, Devon ', *PDAS* 24 (1967), 41

23. Hillsborough hillfort, Ilfracombe parish (SS 533 478)

Hillsborough is a promontory fort built on the forward slope of a headland 60m–120m high which projects boldly into the Bristol Channel east of Ilfracombe, margined by cliffs 30m–60m high. There are natural harbours at its base on either side at Hele and Ilfracombe, which afford some shelter and where boats can be beached. On a clear day the South Wales coast is visible from Worm's Head in Gower to Barry and inland to the Brecon Beacons.

Regrettably the hillfort defences are badly overgrown. These consist of two lines of low ramparts strength-ened by scarping, close together on the west side, but diverging on the east, where there are two inturned entrances some 60m apart.

⚐ Public park. Accessible by Coast Path from Ilfracombe to Hele. Best visited in winter or spring when the bracken and undergrowth are down. Car park beside new swimming pool.

🖎 Whybrow, C. 'Some Multivallate Hillforts on Exmoor and in North Devon', *PDAS* 25 (1967), 1–18, Fig. 9.

24. Hunter's Tor hillfort, Lustleigh parish (SX 761 823) – Plate 8

Situated on the hilltop at 320m beside the granite Hunter's Tor, this triple-ramparted hillfort has been badly damaged by stone robbing for field walls and by ploughing. The site is well defended by steep slopes to the west and north, but with an easy approach from the south-east across Lustleigh Common.

The two inner enclosures were proba-bly stone-walled and have been robbed for a field wall and were per-haps unfinished; the third, probably a later addition, was defended by a bank and ditch, ploughed down on the east side but visible in the pasture field. The best surviving feature is the embanked stone-lined entrance

Plate 8: *Hunter's Tor hillfort (Site No.24)* (F.M.Griffith, Devon County Council)

way 20m long, with knobbed terminals linking the inner and middle enclosures [Fig. 5]. The outer enclosure was entered through an 8m wide gap facing south-east.

Ⓧ Part Lustleigh Common, part private ownership. Access by public footpath from Pecks Farm or Lustleigh Cleave.

🖝 Silvester, R. J. and Quinnell, N. V. 'Unfinished hillforts on the Devon Moors', *PDAS* 51 (1993), 17–22.

25. Huntsham Castle, Huntsham parish (SS 991 179)

A medium-sized hillfort in the rolling upland between the Exe and Lowman rivers, north of Tiverton and 1.5 kilometres south west of Huntsham village.

The defences surround the 264m high hill summit with good views in all directions; they consist of a rampart, 2–3m high, and a broad ditch now partly filled and used as a farm track. The entrance was on the lower north-west side which is wooded and where there are two small quarries. The interior, some 200m across, is in grass but was formerly ploughed.

Ⓧ Privately owned. Permission to visit may be requested at Huntsham Castle Farm on the Huntsham Road nearby.

26. Loddiswell Rings, Loddiswell parish (SX 720 520) – Fig. 23, Plate 2. (also known as Blackdown Rings)

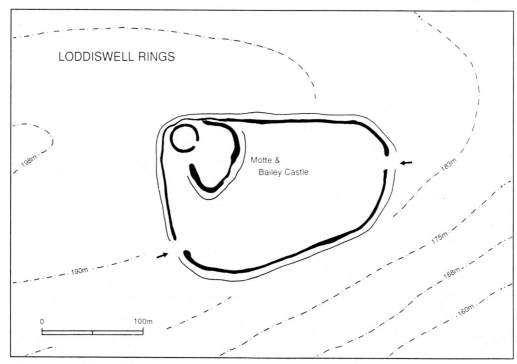

Fig. 23: *Loddiswell Rings*

A large hillfort on the crest of the Blackdown ridge 185m high above and to the west of the river Avon and about 1.5 kilometres north of Loddiswell village. A ridgeway from the head of the Avon estuary to Dartmoor passes close to the site. A Norman motte and bailey timber castle was inserted in the 11th or 12th century AD into the north-west corner of the hillfort.

The Iron Age fortifications consist of a massive rampart up to 1.7m high and a deep ditch which enclose an oval area of about 2 hectares, sloping gently south. On the lower side, the outer face of the rampart has been sharply cut back making a ledge above the lower rock-cut ditch, probably Norman alterations. There is also a counter-scarp bank, surmounted by a modern hedge.

There are two entrances on opposite sides of the hillfort, both widened for farm traffic; the eastern one retains one of its original inturns [Fig. 4]. The interior, now under grass, has been frequently ploughed in the past: it could have been used by the Normans for an encampment whilst building their motte and bailey castle, but nothing is recorded of the castle's history.

⚑ Owned by the Arundell Charity, with public access and car park. Interpretation panels on site.

🕮 Wilson-North, W. R. and Dunn, C. J.'"The Rings", Loddiswell: A New Survey by the Royal Commission on the Historical Monuments of England', *PDAS* 48 (1990), 87–100.

27. Membury Castle, Membury parish (ST 282 029) – Fig. 24.

This medium-sized hillfort is situated on a 200m high point above Membury village on the ridge of the Upper Greensand north of the junction of the rivers Yarty and Axe. The hill here is capped with broken chert and clay, and its steep sides provided good natural defence as well as access to traffic from the ridgeway.

The hillfort is defended by a single rampart 2m high, dug from soil quarried internally and enclosing 1.3 hectares. Although there is much scattered chert on its surface, no remains of stone walling or of an external ditch are visible. There are two entrances: on the east side the

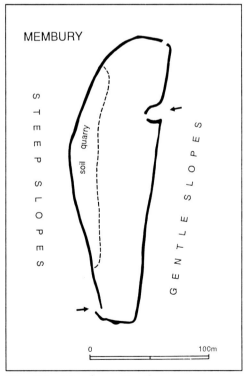

MEMBURY

STEEP SLOPES

soil quarry

GENTLE SLOPES

0   100m

Fig. 24: *Membury Castle*

rampart ends are deeply inturned (13.5m long and 12.3m apart) forming a small forecourt in front of the original gate, now blocked by a field bank. Two small pits on the south side are probably later diggings for chert.

The second entrance, now a public footpath, is at the narrow south-west corner where the rampart ends expand and project forward. The interior on the gently rounded hilltop is now in pasture but was formerly ploughed.

🏃 Privately owned; accessible by public footpath from the road below on the west.

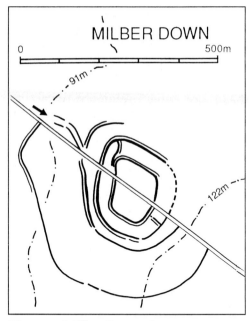

Fig. 25: *Milber Down Camp*

28. Milber Down Camp,
Coffinswell parish (SX 883 698) – Fig 25, Plate 9.

The hillfort on Milber Down is a fine example of a hill-slope fort, constructed on the northern slopes of a 150m high tract of upland between the Teign estuary and the Aller brook, about a kilometre south-east of Newton Abbot. The road to St. Mary-church bisects the fort and the eastern half is now obscured by Castle Plantation and is partly ploughed out, but is visible on the air photograph. Though there are fine views towards Dartmoor to the north, the position is indefensible being 35m below the hilltop, with a further 30m fall internally.

The fort consists of three concentric sub-rectangular enclosures: the inner-most is 116m by 96m in extent, the second and third are narrow strips 10m to 25m wide, each being defended by a substantial rampart and ditch. In addition there was a large outer enclosure probably for cultivation, bounded by a low bank, now damaged and incomplete.

The entrance to the fortifications was on the lower north-west side, facing towards the nearest water supply, the Aller brook. It began as an embanked track 7m wide across the outer enclosure, probably a drove-way for stock to prevent damage to cultivation. The gateways to the inner zones have been destroyed by the modern road.

Excavations in 1937–38 showed that the central and second enclosures were occupied, though no house foundations were excavated. The inhabitants used hand-made pottery

Plate 9: *Milber Down Camp (Site No. 28): this view was taken in the early 1950s. The hillfort now carries more tree cover on the far side of the road* (Cambridge University Collection)

with curvilinear designs (Glastonbury ware, Fig. 10), characteristic of the local Iron Age after 300 BC. A surprising find of three small bronzes, a bird, a duck and a stag [Fig. 11], came from the upper filling of a ditch, buried in the early first century AD after the fort had been abandoned.

ᛉ Privately owned. Access by public footpath from the St Marychurch road across the south-western half of fort. Finds in Torquay Museum.

◳ Devon Archaeological Society *Milber Down* Field Guide No.1 (1987)
Fox, A., Radford C. A. R., Rogers, E. H. and Shorter, A. H. 'Report on the Excavations at Milber Down', *PDAES* 4 (1948–52), 27–65.

29. Mockham Down Camp, Brayford parish (SS 667 358)

On the summit of Mockham Down at the 300m contour on level ground, there are the conspicuous remains of an oval enclosure. The site is well defended on the north and east by the steep slopes to a tributary of the River Bray.

The hillfort (some 150m in diameter) was defended by a single rampart 2m high and a ditch. The north side, where the original entrance was placed, has been badly damaged by a deep stone quarry. A gap on the east side is probably recent. The site is now in pasture.

ᛉ Privately owned: permission to

visit may be requested from the farm-house. On east side of bye-road running south from A399 at Mockham Down Gate..

30. Musbury Castle, Musbury parish (SY 281 940) – Fig. 26.

A large hillfort (3.4 hectares) constructed at the end of a Greensand spur flanking the Axe valley above and south-east of Musbury village. The site, 170m high, was naturally well defended by steep slopes except for a level approach along the spur from the north where two massive ramparts 40m apart were built and where the entrance was situated on the east side. The associated ditches have been mostly filled in and a counter-scarp bank to the outer rampart levelled, apart from a short length at the north-west end, which continues with the rampart downhill into a conifer plantation.

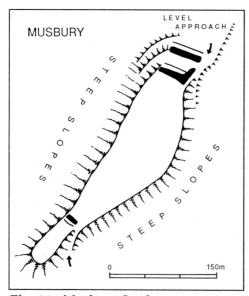

Fig. 26: *Musbury Castle*

At the southern end of the hillfort there is another substantial transverse rampart and ditch, set back 70m from the tip of the spur which is scarped only. There was probably an original entrance here (now much widened), approached by a diagonal track on the east side of the hill.

It is uncertain whether there were low banks along the sides of the hillfort connecting the transverse defences or whether scarping and/or palisades provided sufficient defence at the top of the steep slopes. Along the west side there is a modern boundary bank which cuts into the ends of the ramparts. The interior of the hillfort is now divided by hedge-banks into three grass fields with bracken covering the northern ramparts.

⅄ Privately owned: accessible by public footpath from Musbury church where there is car parking.

31. Myrtleberry North Camp, Lynton and Lynmouth parish (SS 743 487) – Fig. 27.

A small hill-slope enclosure situated at the end of a wooded spur, overlooking a steep sided loop of the East Lyn river, north of Watersmeet. The earthwork can be seen from Windhill promontory fort (see page 55) on the far side of the river.

It is an oval enclosure (74m by 40m) enclosed by a low bank, with a ditch only on the west side and a probable entrance gap at the north-west cor-

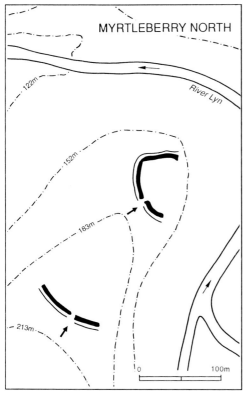

Fig. 27: *Myrtleberry North Camp*

ner. 150m higher up the spur there is a substantial cross-bank and ditch, 80m long, defining an outer enclosure at the foot of a steep slope. The position, though it is hidden away, is indefensible, except on the river sides; it can be compared with Voley Castle (page 54) which is a similar concealed settlement with a cross-bank in the local Iron Age manner.

Mrytleberry South Camp is another small settlement terraced into the hillside, with four or five probable house sites, 300m south of the cross-bank; its date is uncertain, probably medieval.

♟ Owned by National Trust. Public access by footpath (¹/₂ mile) from Hilsford Bridge. National Trust car park at junction of the A39/B3223.

🖙 Whybrow, C. 'Some Multivallate Hillforts on Exmoor and in North Devon', *PDAS* 25 (1967), 8–9

32. Noss Camp, Kingswear parish (SX 888 537) – Fig. 28.

An outstanding hill-slope fort on the east bank of the river Dart 120m above and about a kilometre distant from Noss Point. It is built on the upper slopes of a spur between two steep-sided valleys. The main enclosure trails steeply downhill for 30–40m; it is defended by a single rampart and broad ditch, reinforced on the upper side by a second line across the spur. The entrance is on the east side probably with a half in-turn, but obscured by a hedgebank.

There was probably an outer enclosure higher up the spur, formed by a rampart now incorporated in a hedgebank, and completed by lateral fences or palisades. Now in grass, formerly ploughed.

♟ Privately owned but visible in the distance from the A379 road to Kingswear ferry.

🖙 Fox, A. 'Hill-slope forts and related earthworks in South West England and South Wales', *Archaeological Journal* 109 (1953), 15-16

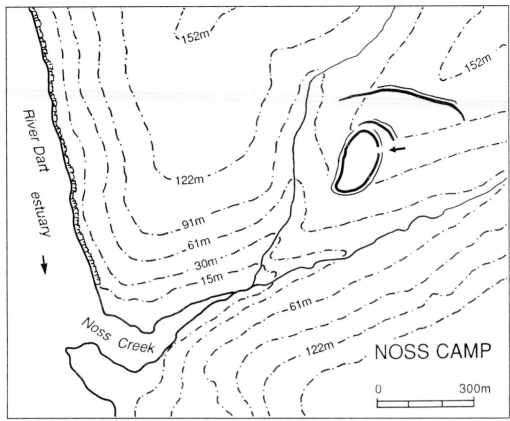

Fig. 28: *Noss Camp*

33. Posbury Camp, Crediton Hamlets parish (SX 809 972) – Fig. 29.

Formerly an impressive multivallate hillfort on the 175m high watershed between the Culvery and Yeo rivers, four kilometres south of Crediton. The soil is Culm clay and sandstone.

The three close-set ramparts and ditches are well preserved in a belt of woodland on the lower south side; the innermost, 8.5m on the scarp and 5m high, continues up the west side but the ditch and middle rampart have been flattened by ploughing and are barely visible in the adjoining

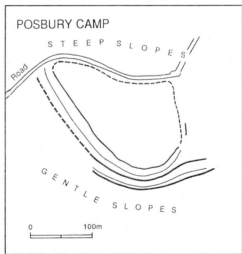

Fig. 29: *Posbury Camp*

field. The outermost rampart diverges and terminates at either end. On the east side all traces of the defences

46

have gone but a substantial hedge-bank is likely to mark the line, continuing on the north side above the narrow lane. The interior is in pasture, sloping gently southwards; no entrance can be located. The triple close-set ramparts are unique in Devon west of the Exe.

ⵣ Privately owned. Lane skirts north side.

34. Prestonbury Castle,
Drewsteignton parish (SX 747 900) – Fig. 30, Plate 10.

Sited on a 220m hilltop overlooking the Teign gorge at Fingle Bridge, Prestonbury is a dramatic hillfort of the multiple enclosure type, built in two periods.

The first hillfort consisted of a circular enclosure on the summit with a crescentic annexe on the east side, perhaps unfinished. The inner zone was probably walled with the local Culm stone on the edge of the gorge, supplemented on the other sides by soil quarried internally. The entrance facing east was a simple gap between

Plate 10: *Prestonbury Castle (Site No.34) is sited on a prominent hilltop overlooking the Teign gorge. The original hilltop defences were strengthened by a later outer rampart (foreground and see Fig.30).* (Cambridge University Collection)

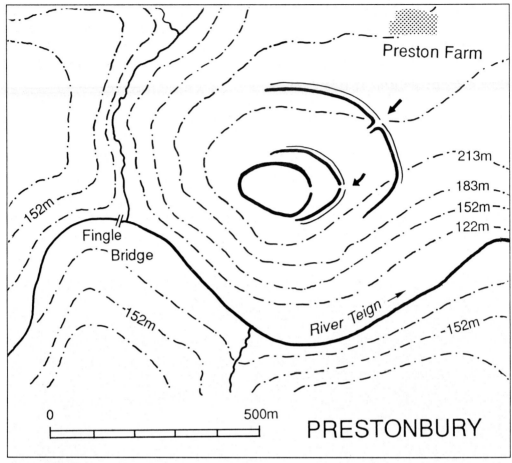

Fig. 30: *Prestonbury Castle*

thickened rampart ends. The annexe has a small-scale rampart dug from an external ditch, but the defences fade out on a natural scarp to the west and were not joined up to the inner zone. The entrance is a 3.5m gap.

In the second period, the hillfort was extended 150m downhill where a massive rampart and ditch were constructed across the neck below Preston Farm, with a deep inturned entrance 20m long [Fig. 5]. The earthwork curves around the hillside westward but fades out. The enclo-sure probably held stock and was completed by a palisade.

🛈Privately owned. Access is permitted from Preston Farm. Parking on road or at Fingle Bridge.

🕮 Fox, A. 'Hill-slope forts and related earthworks in South West England and Wales', *Archaeological Journal* 109(1953), 10–14.

35. Roborough Castle, Shirwell parish (SS 569 353) – Fig. 31. (also known as Burridge hillfort)

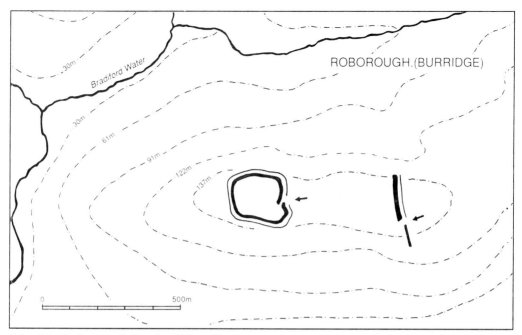

Fig. 31: *Roborough Castle, Shirwell*

This hillfort, with an outwork of south-western type, is situated at 140m on the crest of a steep-sided ridge between the River Yeo and Bradiford Water, some three kilometres north-east of Barnstaple. The enclosure is approximately 100m square with rounded corners and was defended by a substantial rampart and ditch, best preserved in woodland on the west side. On the south the defences have been lowered by ploughing; elsewhere the rampart is incorporated in the hedgebanks and the ditch filled in. The entrance is slightly inturned and faces east but is obscured by a hedgebank.

Some 400m east along the ridge there is a massive cross–bank and ditch 2m high extending between the steep slopes; there was probably an entrance on the line of the present ridge road to Shirwell. It probably defined a large stock enclosure, similar to those at Burley Wood or Prestonbury.

It has been suggested that this Iron Age hillfort was reoccupied in the late 9th or 10th century AD by the Saxons as a defence against the Danes and is to be identified with the site of *Pilton*, listed in the *Burghal Hidage* document, before the focus of Saxon settlement was transferred to Barnstaple; see also Halwell for another example. (Page 35).

⚔ Privately owned. Visible in the grass fields north of the Burridge road from Barnstaple to Shirwell.

☜ Griffith, F. *Devon's Past – An Aerial View* (1988), 71, Plate 56.
    Whybrow, C. 'Some Multivallate Hillforts on Exmoor and in North Devon', *PDAS* 25 (1967), 3

36. Roborough Castle, Lynton and Lynmouth parish (SS 731 460)

A ringwork, 63m internal diameter, on the northern lower slopes of Exmoor and 300m above the steep slopes to the Hoare Oak Water. The earthwork consists of a bank and ditch, 1.25m to 2m high, with an entrance facing south-east, widened by ploughing. Now in grass.

⚔ Privately owned. Narrow lane and public footpath from Barbrook across Stock Common skirts south side of site.

37. Shoulsbury Castle, Brayford/Challacombe parishes (SS 706 391) – Plate 11.

A sub-rectangular enclosure of 1.6 hectacres situated on high ground (470m) on the western fringe of Exmoor, two kilometres south-east of Challacombe and east of the River Bray. The site commands fine views of Bodmin Moor, Dartmoor and South Wales.

The fortifications are small-scale, consisting of an inner rampart 1.5m to 2m high with an accompanying ditch on three sides; the lower south side rests on a natural scarp. There is one entrance with a causeway in the centre of the west side and another possible one on the south-east corner. A second line of bank and ditch at varying distances from the inner defences surrounds the upper portion of the hillfort and is probably unfinished. A possible barrow or hut circle was excavated in 1906 in the interior but nothing was found.

The site has no natural defences and is likely to be a stock enclosure connected with summer grazing on the

Plate 11: *Shoulsbury Castle (Site No.37) occupies a prominent site on the western flanks of Exmoor* (Cambridge University Collection)

high moorland; not necessarily Iron Age in date.

🏠Privately owned. Located above narrow road from Five Cross Way to Mole's Corner.

📖 Silvester, R.J. and Quinnell, N.V. 'Unfinished hillforts on the Devon Moors', *PDAS* 51(1993),27–28
    Whybrow, C 'Some Multivallate Hillforts on Exmoor and in North Devon', *PDAS* 25 (1967),16–17

38. Sidbury Castle, Sidmouth parish (SY 128 913) – Fig. 32.

A fine large hillfort of four hectares on the west side of the Sid valley, built on a 170m high knob at the end of a Greensand spur, overlooking the narrow Sidbury to Ottery roads.

The defences consist of an earth rampart quarried internally, a scarp, and a deep ditch with a substantial counter-scarp bank. These follow the contour round the edge of the steep bracken covered hillsides and are best preserved in the woodland at the east end of the spur. The interior is in grass with a small pond on the north side, perhaps made from an ancient spring, formerly a water supply for the hillfort.

The single entrance faces west: the

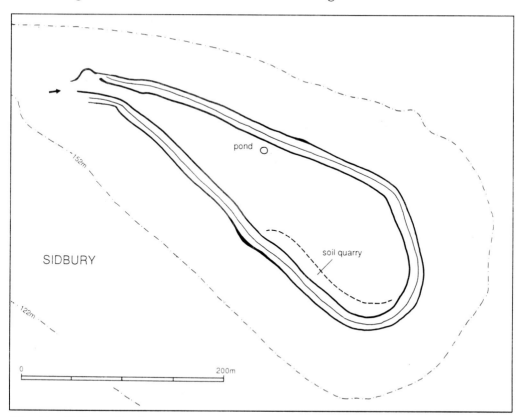

Fig. 32: *Sidbury Castle*

external 50m long passageway is exceptional [Fig. 5]. It is formed from an extension of the main rampart and ditch running steeply downhill and ending on a scarped platform. On the south side, the main ditch finishes, but the rampart is expanded probably to make a fighting platform before continuing downhill. A hole full of slingstones 'enough to fill a wheelbarrow' was found hereabouts in 1864 by workmen breaking up the ground. The passageway has now been deepened by erosion but it seems likely that it included a gateway at both ends.

♟ Privately owned. No public access.

39. Stanborough Camp, Halwell parish (SX 773 517)

A well-preserved circular enclosure, 100m in diameter situated on a rounded 200m high hill-top approached by a ridgeway from the coast at Slapton. The earthwork is in a grass field, formerly ploughed, adjoining the Stanborough Hundred Hotel. It consists of a substantial rampart 2m high and ditch; in places the base of the bank has been cut back and stone-faced and the ditch has been ploughed in. The entrance faced west, a simple gap, enlarged and then partly blocked for a farm track.

♟ Privately owned, adjacent to the Stanborough Hundred Hotel on the A381 Totnes/Kingsbridge Road.

40. Stock Castle, Lynton and Lynmouth parish (SS 718 469)

A small ringwork 45m in diameter on the northern lower slopes of Exmoor at the 290m contour and east of the West Lyn river. The earthworks consist of a bank 1m high and ditch with an entrance facing south. The ditch has been ploughed in on the west side and the entrance gap widened. The interior is now in grass.

♟ Privately owned. Visible from the narrow lane from Barbrook.

41. Stockland Great Castle, Stockland parish (ST 226 026)
– Fig. 33.

This strong hillfort is situated on the eastern side of Stockland Hill, part of an upper Greensand ridge between the Umborne brook and the Yarty river. Only the northern half of the fort survives; the remainder was levelled in the mid nineteenth cen-

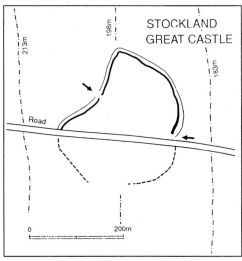

Fig. 33: *Stockland Great Castle*

tury and ploughed in. The site is 20m below a ridge-way and the defences are concealed in a belt of trees. The bye-road to Broadhayes House now bisects the hillfort.

Since this is on a slope site, there were no natural defences, the single rampart and ditch with a counterscarp bank being therefore exceptionally massive. They measure 8-11m on the scarp and 23m overall and include many small pieces of broken chert scattered on the surface, though no remains of a walled revetment can be seen.

There were two entrances; one on the east where the rampart turns inwards beside the road, the other on the west by a causeway across the ditch, much enlarged recently, and through a gap in the rampart. Slingstones were recorded from plough soil in the interior by P. O. Hutchinson in 1868. Some traces of the defences can still be seen in the pasture fields south of the road.

🏹 Privately owned. Visible from the bye-road to Broadhayes House, which bisects the site.

🡒 Griffith, F. *Devon's Past – An Aerial View* (1988), 99, Plate 84.

42. Stockland Little Castle, Stockland parish (ST 230 036)

A ringwork, 100m internal diameter, defended by a single rampart and ditch, partly ploughed in. Some traces of a dry stone revetment on the internal face were recorded by P. O.Hutchinson in 1868. Entrance gap faces south-east. For similar sized ringworks, compare Castle Dyke (Ashcombe), Burridge (Chawleigh) and Stanborough.

🏹 Privately owned.

43. Stoke Hill Camp, Stoke Canon parish (SX 926 957)

This medium-sized hillfort is situated at 150m on the western side of Stoke Hill, above the steep wooded slopes of the Exe valley and south of Stoke Farm. It was formerly part of a golf course, now pasture. The soil is Culm clay and shillet.

The overall enclosure of more than two hectares was defended by a single rampart and ditch, much reduced by ploughing except on the north-west in a belt of trees where the rampart stands some 3m high above the silted ditch. The entrance between slightly incurved rampart ends faces the easy line of approach from the east. Excavation in 1935 by C.A.R. Radford showed that the base of the rampart was faced with turf on both sides. Only 'one piece of first century AD pottery' was found as well as some iron slag and two slingstones.

🏹 Privately owned. Public footpath from Stoke Hill Farm or from the top of Stoke Valley Road runs along east side of site.

🡒 Radford, C. A. R. 'Stoke Hill Camp' *PDAES* 3 (1937–47), 24–32.

44. Voley Castle, Parracombe parish
(SS 655 462) – Fig. 34.

This little enclosure was built on a narrow terrace on the steep east-facing slope of Heale Down 60m above the Heddon river valley. The position is indefensible, being over-looked from the 290m high hill above.

The earthwork is a circular bank and ditch, 60m in internal diameter with a simple entrance facing south. There is a cross-bank and ditch 65m long, with an entrance in line with that of the main enclosure, to which the earthwork was probably attached by a fence or palisade to make an outer stock enclosure.

Voley Castle resembles Myrtleberry North Camp, another small hillfort with a cross-bank and in a similar position above the East Lyn river (see page 44). Beacon Castle, another small ringwork (SS 664 460; privately owned), is visible from Voley on the hill top beyond the Heddon valley.

A Privately owned. Visible from foot-path on Heale Down.

Silvester, R.J. 'Forts and Farms: the Iron Age in Devon', in Devon County Council *Archaeology of the Devon Landscape* (1981), 49, Plate 5.5.
Whybrow, C 'Some Multivallate Hillforts on Exmoor and in North Devon' *PDAS* 25 (1967), 13–14

45. Wasteberry Camp, Brixton Parish (SX 572 539) – Fig. 35.

A large hillfort of south-western type, situated on a 75m hill-top above the steep wooded slopes to the Silver Lake stream flowing south to Brixton. It is defended by two lines of sub-

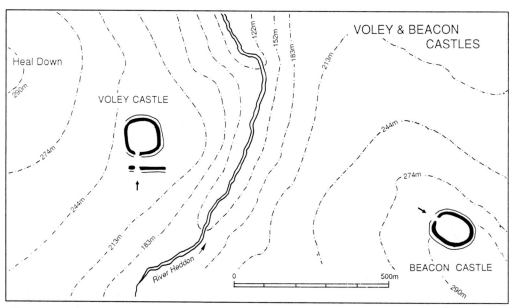

Fig. 34: *Voley and Beacon Castles*

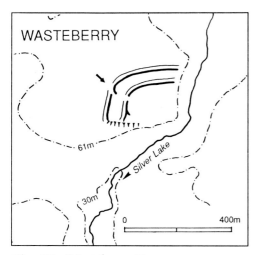

Fig. 35: *Wasteberry Camp*

46. Windhill hillfort, Lynton and Lynmouth parish SS 740 493)
– Plate 12.

A magnificent promontory fort on the North Devon coast, two kilometres east of Lynmouth where it crosses the A39 main road. It defends the 240m summit of Windhill by a massive rampart 3m high, deep ditch and small counter-scarp bank facing east. The earthwork extends 400m seaward from the steep slopes of the East Lyn valley, diminishing in size north of the main A39 road .

stantial ramparts and ditches 45-50m apart and an outer counter-scarp bank, which curve around the hill ending at the steep slopes, though linked by scarping at the south end. The entrances to the two enclosures face north-west; the outer is flanked by a half inturn and a knobbed rampart end 3m high, the inner by thickened ramparts only. A third line, 30m within, consists of a bank, stone-faced and ditched internally; it is thought to belong to the deer park of the 18th century Lyneham House.

Well preserved in grass fields although much of the ditches and the counterscarp are ploughed down or filled in.

🏃 Privately owned.

🕮 Woolner, D. and Woolner, A. 'Waste Berry, Brixton', *Transactions of the Devonshire Association* 88 (1956), 86.

There is an entrance from the east at the highest point, a simple gap, with some stonework visible. Although there is a low bank for a short distance along the south side above the river, there is no indication of a terminal rampart to show how much of the 60 hectares of the hilltop was occupied. Control of the sheltered landings at the mouth of the River Lyn would have been important to the inhabitants.

It is possible that there was a reoccupation of this Iron Age promontory fort by the West Saxons in the 9th Century AD if it can be identified with the *Arx Cynuit* mentioned in the *Anglo Saxon Chronicle* and Asser's *Life of King Alfred.* Here the Danes besieged the Christian Saxons in AD 878 and were defeated and their leader Hubba killed.

🏃 Owned by the National Trust. Car park at Countisbury church. Public access by footpath from the A39.

Plate 12: *The massive rampart on Windhill (Site No.46) extends for 400m to protect this hilltop on the Exmoor coast* (F.M.Griffith, Devon County Council)

📖 Stevenson, W H (ed.) *Asser's Life of King Alfred* (1904), 138 and 262.

47. Woodbury Castle, Woodbury parish (SY 032 873) – Fig. 36.

A conspicuous hill-top fort, on the crest (175m) of a ridge of the Bunter Pebble Beds on Woodbury Common, two kilometres east of Woodbury village. The B3180 runs through the fort, passing through the two entrances.

The main enclosure of 2 hectares is defended by a massive steep rampart and deep ditch, supplemented on the north and east sides by a substantial counter-scarp bank. On the west side the defences are doubled and the end of the second rampart is expanded to create a fighting platform beside the northern entrance. The main rampart turns inwards to flank the southern entrance, now under the road. Other gaps are modern.

60m to the north there is another smaller rampart and ditch across the ridge, extending to Soldiers' Well, a spring on the western side, which probably served as the water supply for the hillfort. On the southern and western sides there are intermittent earthworks that are earlier than the

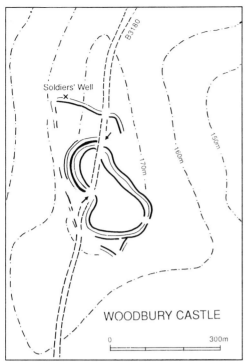

Fig. 36: *Woodbury Castle*

main hillfort. The interior is now open woodland, partly occupied by a private cottage.

Limited excavation of a narrow strip alongside the road in 1971 by Henrietta Quinnell showed that a palisaded enclosure pre-dated the defences. The inner rampart was found to have a turf revetment at the back and was topped by a timber breastwork; subsequently it was heightened and the breastwork renewed. At the northern entrance, the rampart ends were revetted with timber and later strengthened with stone, whilst in the interior there were post-holes indicating rectangular timber buildings, possibly granaries. Finds were very few but the pottery suggested that the defences were completed before 300 BC. [Fig. 3].

🔏 Sited on common land in the ownership of Clinton Devon Estates. Car parks adjoin the hillfort on the north and south sides, where the Devon Archaeological Society has set up interpretation panels.

🕮 Devon Archaeological Society *Woodbury Castle* Field Guide No.2 (1987)
Miles, H 'Excavations at Woodbury Castle, East Devon, 1971' *PDAS* 33 (1975), 183–208.

48. Wooston Castle, Moretonhampstead parish (SX 765 896) – Fig. 37.

An unusual hill-slope fort of multiple enclosure (south-western) type situated on the wooded slopes above the Teign gorge, about two kilometres upstream from Clifford Bridge.

The main enclosure lies hidden away on the shoulder of a steep-sided bluff at about 180m, well above the precipitous river gorge to the north. It is defended not only by scarping on the north and east sides but by a sizeable rampart and ditch starting on the west and then crossing the bluff, facing south; it includes a central entrance gap with an out-turned rampart end. 100m farther south there is a second transverse line of rampart and ditch defensively sited, ending on the steep slopes on either side, but with a small later extension westward towards a spring. There is a central entrance gap, screened by a heightened out-turn of the rampart, recently cut through by a track.

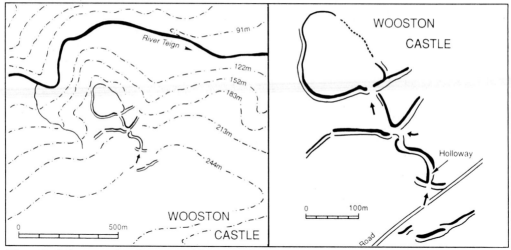

Fig. 37: *Wooston Castle: general location (left) and site plan showing entrance arrangements (right)*

From here a remarkable deep holloway winds up the steep hillside, ending beside the modern road from Clifford Bridge, where it is flanked by short lengths of earthwork on either side. Higher up again there are similar intermittent (? damaged) earthworks below the road to Wooston Farm, and over 60m higher than the main enclosure.

It is clear that only the two lower zones were defensible, though at a tactical disadvantage from the slope. The purpose of the outer earthworks is obscure; probably they are secondary constructions, which could be extended by timber fences to make enclosures for stock or for cultivation, using the holloway as a bye-pass.

Privately owned and recently partly cleared by Lonsdale Forestry. Approached by steep narrow lanes from Clifford Bridge or Moretonhampstead. Limited parking and access by footpath.

Fox, A 'Hill-slope forts and related earthworks in South West England and South Wales' *Archaeological Journal* 109 (1953), 14–15
Silvester, R J 'The Relationship of First Millennium Settlement to the Upland Areas of the South West' *PDAS* 37 (1979), 182.

Illustration credits

The author and publisher are grateful to the following individuals and organisations who kindly provided photographs and illustrations for use in this book: Devon Archaeological Society – Plate 1, Figs 3, 4, 8 and 11; Exeter University, Department of History and Archaeology – Fig 10; Devon Record Office – back cover illustration from Hutchinson's diaries; Devon County Council, Environment Department (Frances Griffith) – Plates 2, 3, 5, 7, 8, 12; Devon County Council, Environment Department (W. Horner) – front cover illustration; National Museum of Wales (Dr Elin M. Jones) – Fig 7; Cambridge University Collection – Plates 4, 6, 9, 10, 11.

Record your Hillfort visits

A good number of the hillforts in the Gazetteer are accessible to the public (see page 20). You can use this page to keep a record of the ones you visit.

Hillfort Name   **Date of Visit**

1   . . . .

2   . . . .

3   . . . .

4   . . . .

5   . . . .

6   . . . .

7   . . . .

8   . . . .

9   . . . .

10   . . . .

11   . . . .

12   . . . .

13   . . . .

14   . . . .

15   . . . .

16   . . . .

17   . . . .

18   . . . .

19   . . . .

20   . . . .